SilverTip

Lakes and Oceans

by Ashley Kuehl

Consultant: Jordan Stoleru,
Science Educator

BEARPORT
PUBLISHING

Minneapolis, Minnesota

Credits

Cover and title page, © coberschneider/Getty Images; 3, © Ruslan Suseynov/Shutterstock; 4–5, © Wildnerdpix/Shutterstock; 7T, © ismailbasdas/AdobeStock; 7B, © ismailbasdas/AdobeStock; 9, © DOERS/Shutterstock; 10–11, © VicPhotoria/Shutterstock; 13, © Piotr Piatrouski/Shutterstock; 15, © Yvonne Baur/Shutterstock; 16–17, © Locomotive74/Shutterstock; 19, © Viacheslav Lopatin/Shutterstock; 20–21, © Anton Balazh/Shutterstock; 23, © Oksana Shchelkanova/Shutterstock; 25, © Damsea/Shutterstock; 27, © LightField Studios/Shutterstock; 28T, © wickerwood/Shutterstock; 28B, © mapichai/Shutterstock.

Bearport Publishing Company Product Development Team

President: Jen Jenson; Director of Product Development: Spencer Brinker; Managing Editor: Allison Juda; Associate Editor: Naomi Reich; Associate Editor: Tiana Tran; Art Director: Colin O'Dea; Designer: Kim Jones; Designer: Kayla Eggert; Product Development Assistant: Owen Hamlin

Statement on Usage of Generative Artificial Intelligence

Bearport Publishing remains committed to publishing high-quality nonfiction books. Therefore, we restrict the use of generative AI to ensure accuracy of all text and visual components pertaining to a book's subject. See BearportPublishing.com for details.

Library of Congress Cataloging-in-Publication Data

Names: Kuehl, Ashley, 1977– author.
Title: Lakes and oceans / By Ashley Kuehl.
Description: Minneapolis, Minnesota : Bearport Publishing Company, [2025] | Series: Earth science-landforms: need to know | Includes bibliographical references and index.
Identifiers: LCCN 2023059736 (print) | LCCN 2023059737 (ebook) | ISBN 9798892320498 (library binding) | ISBN 9798892325233 (paperback) | ISBN 9798892321822 (ebook)
Subjects: LCSH: Lakes–Juvenile literature. | Oceans–Juvenile literature. | Glaciers–Juvenile literature.
Classification: LCC GB1603.8 .K84 2025 (print) | LCC GB1603.8 (ebook) | DDC 577.63–dc23/eng/20240104
LC record available at https://lccn.loc.gov/2023059736
LC ebook record available at https://lccn.loc.gov/2023059737

For more information, write to Bearport Publishing, 5357 Penn Avenue South, Minneapolis, MN 55419.

Contents

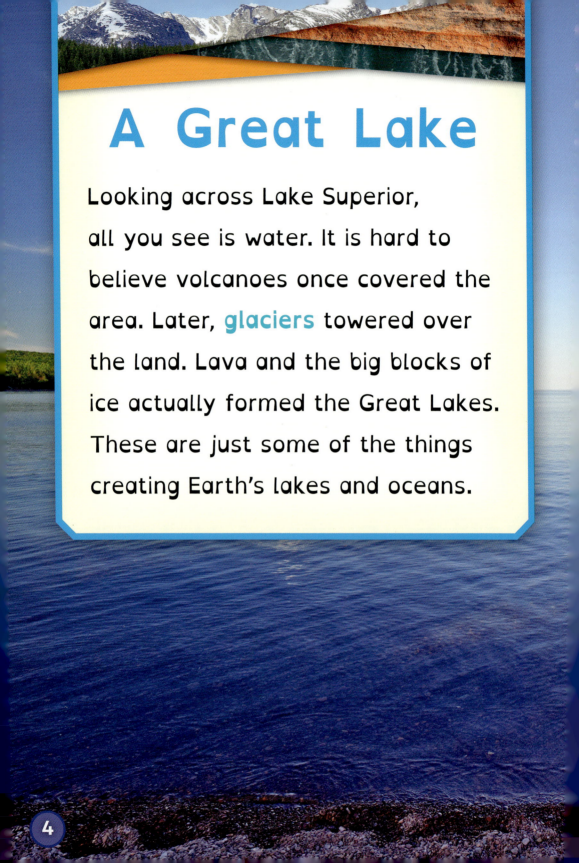

A Great Lake

Looking across Lake Superior, all you see is water. It is hard to believe volcanoes once covered the area. Later, **glaciers** towered over the land. Lava and the big blocks of ice actually formed the Great Lakes. These are just some of the things creating Earth's lakes and oceans.

Many of Earth's modern lakes formed millions or even billions of years ago. Volcanic events that started shaping Lake Superior happened about 1.1 billion years ago.

Lake Superior is one of the world's largest freshwater lakes.

The Supersized Sea

Water covers about 71 percent of Earth. Around 97 percent of the planet's water is in the ocean. This huge body of salt water has been around since there has been liquid water on Earth.

People have given different parts of the ocean different names. However, it is actually one connected landform.

Scientists have been studying the ocean for more than 100 years. However, they haven't gotten very far. The ocean is so large and deep that humans have explored less than 20 percent of it.

ATLANTIC
OCEAN

PACIFIC
OCEAN

ARCTIC OCEAN

INDIAN
OCEAN

SOUTHERN OCEAN

The ocean is more than just seawater and sand. It has landforms along its floor that take similar shapes to the ones on dry land.

The bottom of the ocean is covered in mountain ranges and cliffs. It has large, flat plains and long, deep, narrow holes called trenches.

On average, the ocean is about 12,100 feet (3,700 m) deep. The deepest part is the Mariana Trench. This split in the floor of the Pacific is more than 35,000 ft. (10,000 m) below sea level.

Powerful Plates

What makes the ocean floor uneven? The secret is hidden down deep. Earth's **crust** is made of huge, flat pieces of rock called **tectonic plates**. They are always moving very slowly. As they do, the plates can push up or pull apart the ocean floor.

Earth's tectonic plates fit together a bit like pieces of a puzzle.

When tectonic plates move apart, they may leave cracks. Sometimes, hot **magma** comes from below the crust. It shoots out from between these splits. It hardens into a new **ridge** along the ocean floor.

Keeping it Fresh

Lakes are watery landforms that are smaller than the ocean. They have land all around them.

Unlike the ocean, most lakes hold fresh water. Many are fed by rivers. Others fill up with rainwater or melting ice. A few lakes are salty. They get salt from the land around them.

Lakes are made by nature. A large, human-made body of water is called a **reservoir**. People make reservoirs by blocking flowing water with dams.

Plates, Lava, and Ice

It can take millions of years for lakes to take shape. They can form in a few ways.

As with the ocean floor, the movement of Earth's plates causes changes to the land. Sometimes, this movement makes big holes, or **basins**. Volcanic activity can also create basins.

Sometimes, lakes form in the ocean. A volcano can break through the ocean's surface. Its cooled lava can block off a small part of the ocean, forming a lake.

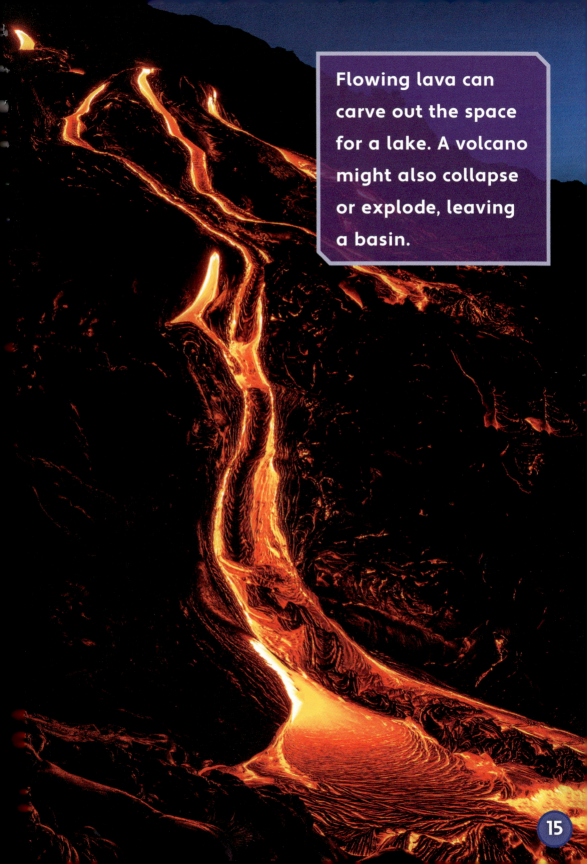

Flowing lava can carve out the space for a lake. A volcano might also collapse or explode, leaving a basin.

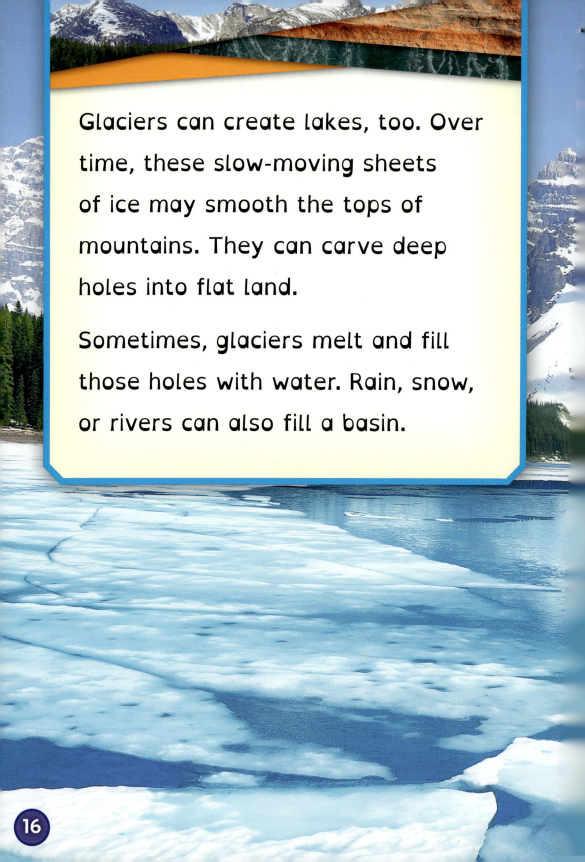

Glaciers can create lakes, too. Over time, these slow-moving sheets of ice may smooth the tops of mountains. They can carve deep holes into flat land.

Sometimes, glaciers melt and fill those holes with water. Rain, snow, or rivers can also fill a basin.

Today, glaciers are melting faster due to climate change. The lakes they form are filling fast. Some are at risk of flooding land nearby.

Always Changing

Millions or billions of years after first forming, lakes and oceans are still changing. Tectonic plates keep moving, affecting the land below the waves. Some underwater mountains get flatter. Others grow higher. As long as tectonic plates keep shifting, the watery floor will keep changing.

The Mid-Atlantic Ridge is a mountain range that is mostly underwater. It is spreading out about 2 inches (5.1 cm) each year.

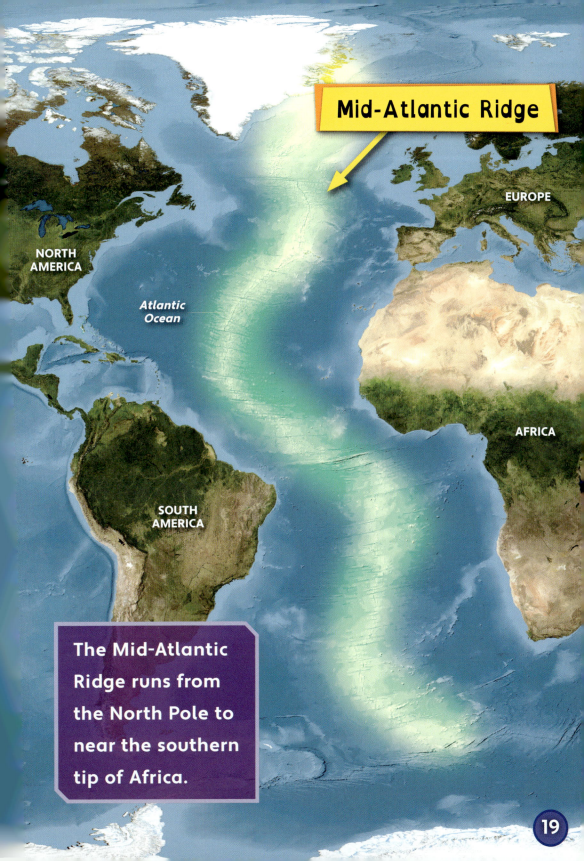

Mid-Atlantic Ridge

EUROPE

NORTH
AMERICA

*Atlantic
Ocean*

AFRICA

SOUTH
AMERICA

The Mid-Atlantic Ridge runs from the North Pole to near the southern tip of Africa.

The water in lakes and oceans is always changing the area around the landforms. Sometimes, water pushes against the shore. It can also flood the land nearby. Both actions break off pieces of the land. The shoreline is constantly being shaped and reshaped by the water.

Flowing ocean waves change
the bottom of the ocean, too.
The water pushes or moves
bits of the ocean floor,
making it flatter or steeper.

Cycling Water

Earth's ocean and lake water is always changing. That is because water moves all around Earth through the water cycle. Water leaves lakes and oceans as a gas. It falls back to the watery landforms below as rain and snow.

During the water cycle, water goes through different states. Energy from the sun turns liquid water into a gas called water vapor. It groups together again in clouds. Water falls back to Earth as liquid rain or solid snow.

Rain falls when clouds get too heavy to hold their water.

Life and Earth's Water

Oceans and lakes are important for life on Earth. Many animals and plants live in these bodies of water. Plants often live near the edges or surface of the water. So do many animals. They need more sunlight. Creatures living deeper need to be used to darkness.

Scientists divide the ocean into zones of depth. The area closest to the surface is called the sunlight zone. It gets lots of light. The deepest area is the hadal zone. It doesn't get any light.

Humans need lakes and oceans, too. We use water from lakes for drinking and farming. We eat plants and animals that live in water. As lakes and the ocean change, so do our interactions with them. This relationship will continue to change as these watery landforms do.

Scientists think the ocean will rise in the near future. They believe lakes will probably get smaller. The land under the water will keep changing, too.

Some people go to lakes and oceans to have fun.

How Glaciers Make Lakes

Some lakes are formed and filled by glaciers.
Here is how that happens.

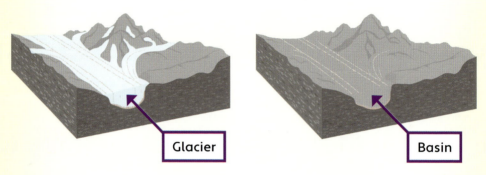

A glacier carves out a basin as it slowly moves across land.

If the glacier ice begins to melt,
it can drip into the basin.

The basin fills with water.
It becomes a lake.

★ SilverTips for REVIEW

Review what you've learned. Use the text to help you.

Define key terms

basin   tectonic plates
glacier   water cycle
ocean floor

Check for understanding

In what ways are lakes and oceans alike? In what ways are they different?

Explain how tectonic plates form and shape Earth's lakes and oceans.

How are Earth's oceans and lakes still changing today?

Think deeper

What part do Earth's oceans and lakes play in your life? How might your life change if the lakes and oceans change in a big way?

★ SilverTips on TEST-TAKING

- **Make a study plan.** Ask your teacher what the test is going to cover. Then, set aside time to study a little bit every day.

- **Read all the questions carefully.** Be sure you know what is being asked.

- **Skip any questions** you don't know how to answer right away. Mark them and come back later if you have time.

Glossary

basins large holes or depressions in the land

crust the hard, outer layer of Earth

glaciers large, slow-moving pieces of ice on land

landform a natural feature on Earth's surface

magma hot melted rock found beneath Earth's
surface

plains large, flat areas of land

reservoir a human-made lake created to store
fresh water

ridge a narrow chain of hills or mountains

tectonic plates huge sheets of rock that make up
Earth's outer crust

trenches long, narrow ditches or cracks in Earth's
surface

Read More

Emminizer, Theresa. *Moving Ice: How the Great Lakes Formed (Earth's History Through Rocks).* New York: PowerKids Press, 2020.

Kuehl, Ashley. *Rivers and Streams (Earth Science–Landforms: Need to Know).* Minneapolis: Bearport Publishing Company, 2025.

Setford, Steve. *Did You Know? Ocean (Did You Know?).* New York: DK, 2022.

Learn More Online

1. Go to **www.factsurfer.com** or scan the QR code below.

2. Enter "**Lakes and Oceans**" into the search box.

3. Click on the cover of this book to see a list of websites.

Index

About the Author

Ashley Kuehl is an editor and writer specializing in nonfiction for young people. She lives in Minneapolis, MN.